Rainbow Songbook

Editor
Alan C. Whitmore

WOOD LAKE BOOKS

Editor: Alan C. Whitmore
Proofreading: Dianne Greenslade
Permissions: Lindy Jones
Cover and interior design: Margaret Kyle
Cover art: Crystal Przybille

We acknowledge the financial support of the Government of Canada through the Book Publishing Industry Development Program for our publishing activities.

At WOOD LAKE BOOKS we practice what we publish, guided by a concern for fairness, justice, and equal opportunity in all of our relationships with employees and customers.

Wood Lake Books Inc. is committed to caring for the environment and all creation. We recycle, reuse and compost, and encourage readers to do the same. Resources are printed on recycled paper and more environmentally friendly groundwood papers (newsprint), whenever possible. A portion of all profit is donated to charitable organizations.

Canadian Cataloguing in Publication Data
Main entry under title:
Rainbow songbook [music]
Songs with piano acc. and chord symbols.
Editor Canadian.
Includes index.
ISBN 1-55145-392-4
1. Songbooks I. Whitmore, Alan C.
M1627.R154 2000   782.42
C00-910460-7

Copyright © 2000 Wood Lake Books Inc.
All rights reserved. No part of this publication may be reproduced – except in the case of brief quotations embodied in critical articles and reviews – stored in an electronic retrieval system, or transmitted in any form or by any means, electronic, mechanical, photocopying, recording, or otherwise, without prior written permission of the publisher or copyright holder.

Published by
Wood Lake Books Inc.
Kelowna, British Columbia, Canada
e-mail: info@woodlake.com
1.250.766.2778
www.joinhands.com

Printing 9 8 7 6 5 4 3 2 1

Printed in Canada by
Transcontinental Printing

Contents

Preface	vii
Arriving Song	1
Blow Out the Candle	32
Clap Your Hands	3
Closing Song	39
Come into God's Presence	37
Come, Lord Jesus	4
Dance with the Spirit	6
Draw the Circle Wide	5
Every Morning Is Easter Morning	7
Everything We Need	9
From You I Receive	8
Get Ready	10
Give Glory to God	11
Glory to God	12
Go Now in Peace	14
God Is Here	13
God Is Like...	15
God Is So Good	17
God Sees the Children	16
Growing in God's Way	18
Halle, Halle, Hallelujah	20
Hands Left and Right	19
I Am Sent by God	21
I Will Sing, I Will Sing	22
Jesus Came a Child Like Me	23
Jesus Came Bringing Us	24
Jesus Loves the Little Children/ Dancing Rainbows	25
Jesus Put This Song into Our Hearts	26
Kind Hands	27
Leaving Song	2
Let's Talk	28
Light One Candle	29
Light Up the Candle	32
Living in the Light	31
Love the Lord Your God	30
Love, Love, Love Your God	33
Love, Love, Love! That's What	34
Magic Penny	35
Make a Joyful Noise	44
May the Hope	36
My Peace	40
My Promise	38
Oh, What a Wonderful Gift	42
One More Step	41
Opening Song	39
Part of the Family	43
Rejoice in the Lord Always	45
Shalom	46
Simple Gifts	48
Sing Alleluia	47
Ten Commandments	49
Thank God	50
The People of God	53
The Spirit in Me	51
The Whole People of God	54
The Whole World	52
This Is My Commandment	55
Three Psalm Settings	61
Turning of the World	57
Walk in the Light	56
Walk with Me	58
We Are the Church	59
What Does the Lord Require?	62
Who Is a Disciple?	60
You Gotta Love	63
Index of Topics & Categories	85

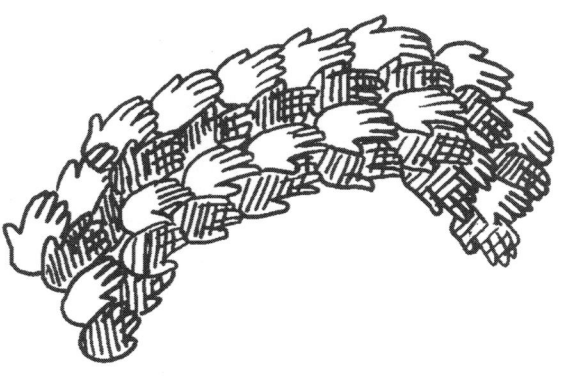

Preface

The *Rainbow Songbook* is the musical culmination of many years of teaching people of all ages about God's love and the redeeming presence of Jesus Christ. It is the end of the rainbow – the gathering together of these songs into one collection.

Music that is intergenerational is important in our lives. We need songs that are easy to sing yet convey truth about our Christian faith that all ages can sing. The songs in *Rainbow* fill this need. The longer songs contain a refrain that even the youngest of our family can learn.

Many of the songs in *Rainbow* help us learn and retell stories from the Bible. Singing the stories of our faith is an excellent way to keep our faith alive. The rhythm and harmony found in songs is very appealing to children and adults. It makes the learning so much more enjoyable.

The collection of songs in *Rainbow* should help to build a musical heritage for our church. There are songs that are familiar and well loved. There are also some which will be new. Sing them all to the glory of God. Allow our faith horizon to grow and strengthen.

Finally, *Rainbow* is a collection of songs that are educational and worshipful. This versatility allows us to integrate education and worship into a rich tapestry called life. Each of these songs will add a new color and texture.

Rainbow is more than a songbook, however. It is a book about community. It is a book that sings about our living together in Christian love and harmony. Sing these songs whenever possible. Sing them when you gather for meetings, for prayer, and for worship. Sing them when you are at home, in the car, or with friends. Express your faith in song. Help the rest of your world to sing along.

Companion tapes and CDs are available with this new songbook. This will allow easier teaching of the songs and also an opportunity for children to just sing along and enjoy using their voices.

There are many people to thank for their participation in this project. Special thanks go to:
- The writers and editors of *The Whole People of God* curriculum resource for much of the material suggested in the sidebars.
- The editorial and prepress teams of Wood Lake Books.
- Donald Schmidt, who dreamed of this book for many years. His help and guidance are greatly appreciated.

Note: We have included actions and/or American Sign Language graphics with some songs. American Sign Language graphics are differentiated from ordinary actions by enclosing them in a box.

Arriving song

Words and music: Flora Litt & Wayne Irwin
Copyright © Flora Litt and Wayne Irwin. Used by permission.

2 Leaving song

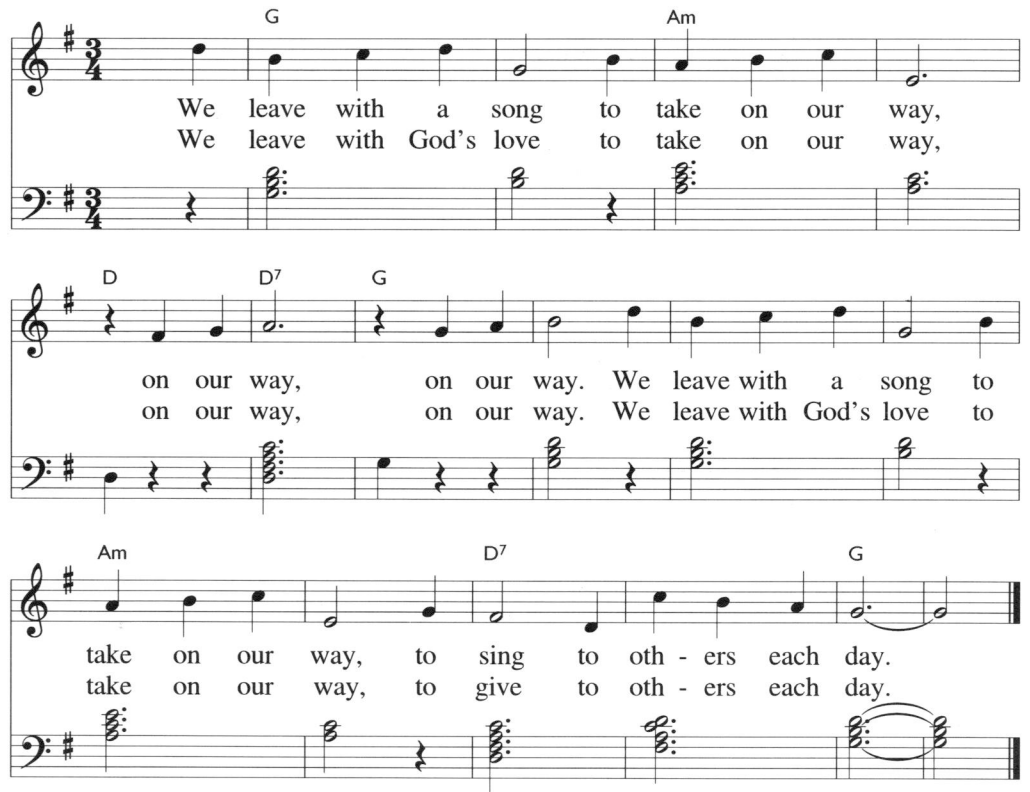

We leave with a song to take on our way,
on our way, on our way. We leave with a song to take on our way, to sing to others each day.

We leave with God's love to take on our way,
on our way, on our way. We leave with God's love to take on our way, to give to others each day.

Words and music: Flora Litt & Wayne Irwin
Copyright © Flora Litt and Wayne Irwin. Used by permission.

Clap your hands

3

This is a zipper song, create your own verses.

Clap your hands and sing to the Lord. Hal-le-lu, hal-le-lu, hal-le-lu-jah.
Snap your fingers sing to the Lord.
Lift your hands and sing to the Lord.

Hal-le-lu-jah, hal-le-lu-jah, hal-le-lu-jah, hal-le-lu-jah, a-men. Hal-le-(men.)

Words and music: Don Moen
Copyright © 1990 Integrity's Hosanna! Music/ASCAP.
All rights reserved. International copyright secured.
Used by permission.

Rainbow Songbook

4 Come, Lord Jesus

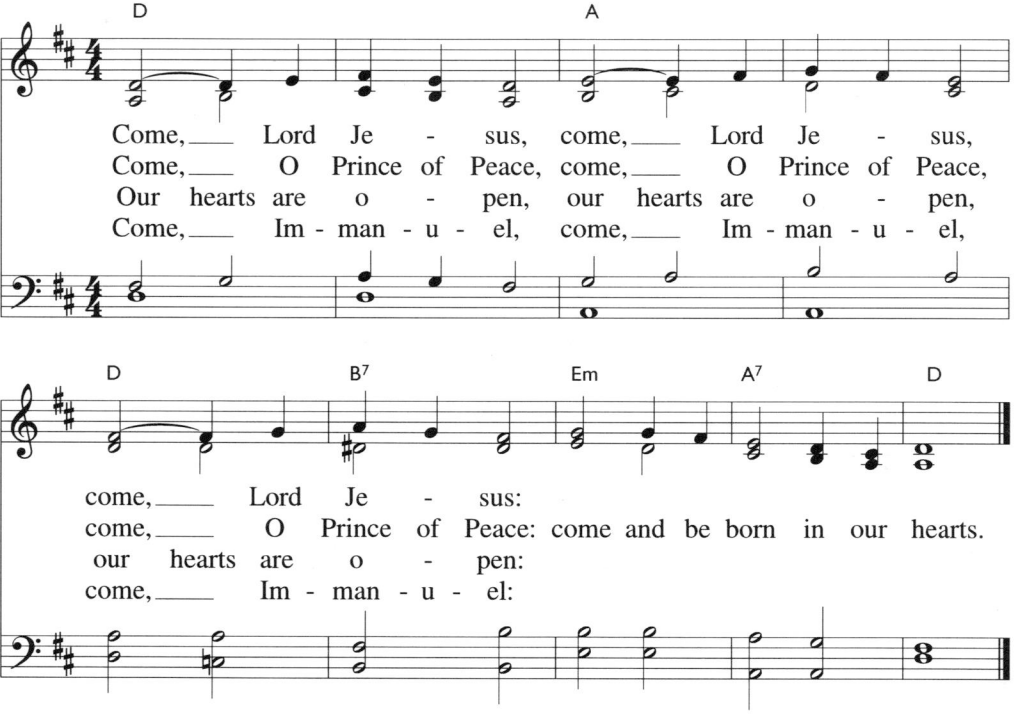

Come,___ Lord Jesus, come,___ Lord Jesus, come,___ Lord Jesus:
Come,___ O Prince of Peace, come,___ O Prince of Peace, come,___ O Prince of Peace: come and be born in our hearts.
Our hearts are o-pen, our hearts are o-pen, our hearts are o-pen:
Come,___ Im-man-u-el, come,___ Im-man-u-el, come,___ Im-man-u-el:

Words and music: Carey Landry
Copyright © 1976 North American Liturgy Resources (NALR), 5536 NE Hassalo, Portland, OR 97213.
All rights reserved. Used by permission of OCP Publications.
Artwork Copyright © Wood Lake Books

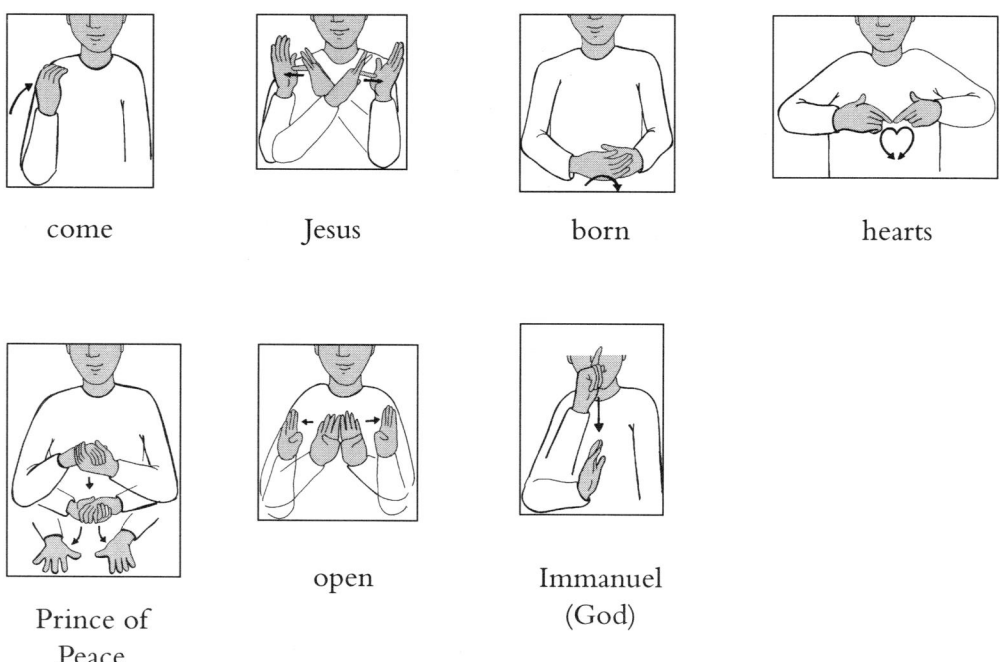

come   Jesus   born   hearts

Prince of Peace   open   Immanuel (God)

Rainbow Songbook

Draw the circle wide

5

continued on next page

Rainbow Songbook

Draw the circle wide (cont'd)

God the still point of the cir - cle round whom all cre - a - tion turns. No-thing lost, but held to - geth - er in God's gra - cious arms.
Let our hearts touch far hor - i - zons, so en - com - pass great and small; Let our lov - ing know no bor - ders, faith - ful to God's call.
Let the dreams we dream be larg - er than we've ev - er dreamed be - fore; Let the dream of Christ be in us, o - pen eve - ry door.

Draw the circle wide (cont'd)

Words and music: Gordon Light, Arr.: Andrew Donaldson
Words and music copyright © 1994 Common Cup Company.
Arr. copyright © 1999 Andrew Donaldson. Used by permission.

6 Dance with the Spirit

This song may be sung at various tempos. When singing this song at a slow tempo, make sure the rhythm is very accented. Percussion will add greatly to the presentation of this song.

Dance with the Spirit (cont'd)

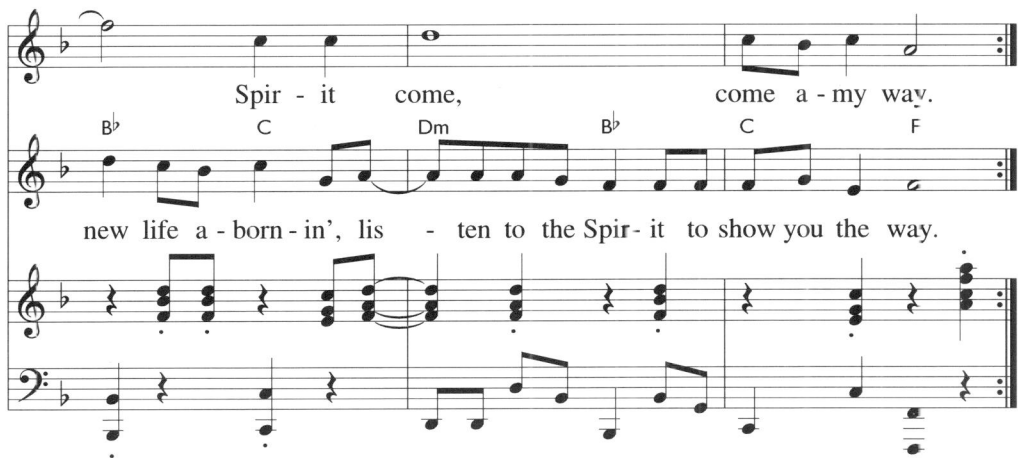

Words and music: Jim Strathdee
Copyright © 1995 Desert Flower Music. Used by permission.

7 Every morning is Easter morning

Every morning is Easter morning (cont'd)

Words and music: Richard Avery & Donald Marsh
Copyright © 1972 by Hope Publishing Company, Carol Stream, IL 60188.
All rights reserved. Used by permission.

From you I receive

Copyright © Christian Aid UK.

9   Everything we need

This is a zipper song. Create your own verses. You may also use the names of the children present to create a new song. (God gives us not just [name], not just [name], not just [name], but everyone we need.)

Words: Sarah Jane Schmidt
Music: Donald Schmidt Arr. Alan Whitmore
Words and music copyright © 1995 Donald Schmidt. Arr. copyright © 1995 Wood Lake Books.

Get ready

10

This song works well with the accompaniment or sung a capella. Use rhythm instruments or finger-snapping and clapping to enhance the presentation. (Thigh-slapping can replace the finger-snapping.)

Begin by getting the congregation snapping (or slapping) a few bars until a good rhythm is established.

Add the words "Get ready" as a bridge between the clap at the end of one bar and the snap at the beginning of the next. Invite people to keep the rhythm going and add the words of the chorus after one or two "GET READY"s. Invite people to keep the rhythm going (including the words GET READY) while a soloist sings the verses.

Count: Phrases of two bars each in 4/4 time as shown in the gray box.

Words and music: Meg Jordan
Arr. Linnea Good
Words and music copyright© Meg Jordan. Arr. copyright © Linnea Good.
Used by permission.

1	and	2	and	3	and	4	and	1	and	2	and etc.
snap		snap		snap		snap/clap		snap		snap	
						GET	READY				

Rainbow Songbook

11   Give glory to God

Sing this song as written or in a "leader-response" form. Everyone should join in singing the "Glory to God" lines. Use a variety of rhythm instruments to give this song even more energy and allow children to participate fully.

Words and music: Donald Schmidt, arr. Michael Bloss
Words and music copyright © 1991 Donald Schmidt.
Arr. copyright © 1998 Wood Lake Books.

Glory to God

12

This is an important song for children under seven. When introducing this song, use a song leader to sing the first part of each line of the verses. Have everyone sing "Praise the name of the Lord." Use percussion to add excitement and encourage participation.

Words and music: Jim Strathdee
Copyright © 1977 Desert Flower Music. Used by permission.

13 God is here

ACCOMPANIMENT 1

This song is especially suited for use by younger children. Use it as a grace before meals or snack time. Add actions where necessary. The two accompaniments provided give variety to the presentation of this song. Learn both of them.

ACCOMPANIMENT 2

Words and music: Donald Schmidt, Accompaniment 1 arr. Michael Bloss
Copyright © 1997 Wood Lake Books. Used by permission.

Go now in peace

14

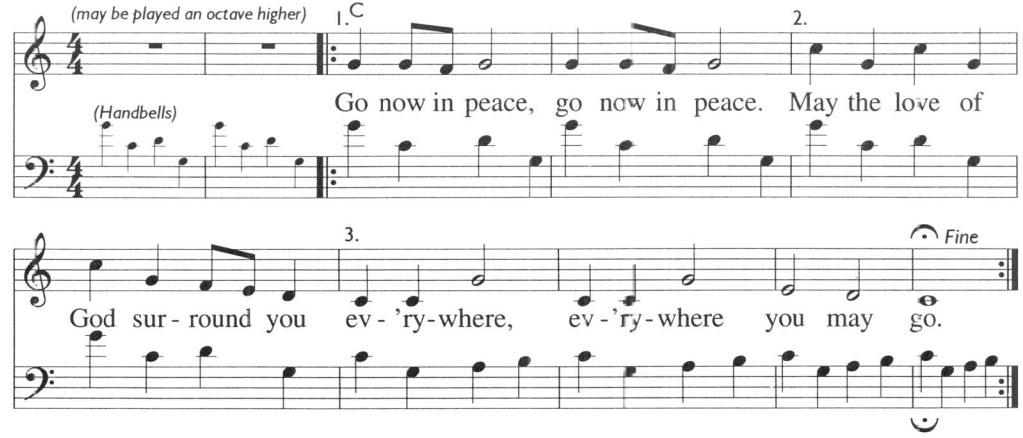

Go now in peace, go now in peace. May the love of
God sur-round you ev-'ry-where, ev-'ry-where you may go.

Use this song after a circle prayer time. Have the group hold hands and look at each other as they sing.

Words and music: Natalie Sleeth
Copyright © 1976 Hinshaw Music, Inc. Used by permission.

God is like

15

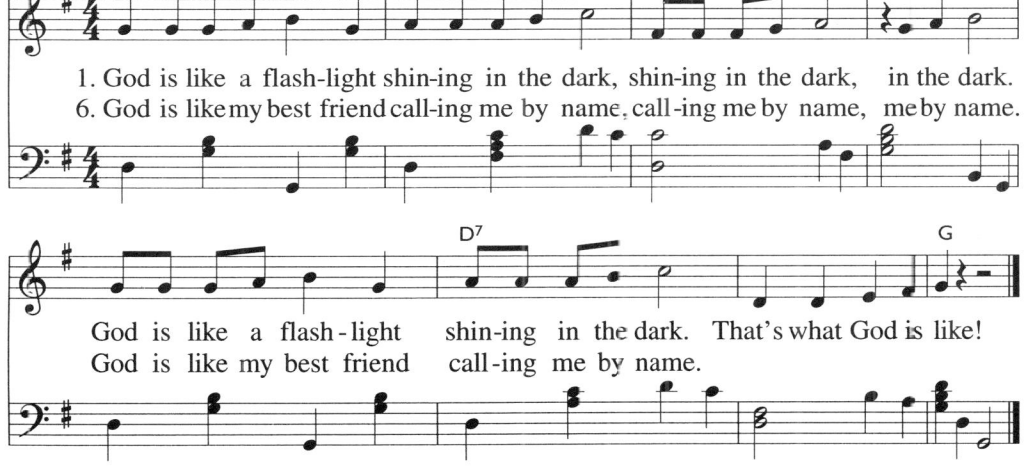

1. God is like a flash-light shin-ing in the dark, shin-ing in the dark, in the dark.
6. God is like my best friend call-ing me by name, call-ing me by name, me by name.

God is like a flash-light shin-ing in the dark. That's what God is like!
God is like my best friend call-ing me by name.

This is a zipper song. Encourage the children to explore their own ideas about God and to write their own verses.

2. God is like a mother giving me a hug.
3. God is like a father saying, "Welcome home."
4. God is like cold water on a hot, dry day.
5. God is like a loaf of bread shared by all around.

Add your own verses.

Words and music: Lesley J. Clare
Copyright © 1990 Lesley J. Clare. Used by permission.

Rainbow Songbook

16 God sees the children

This is an excellent song to help children focus on their feelings around poverty and injustice. It would make an excellent "theme" song for a study about the Third World and how we relate to it.

Rainbow Songbook

God sees the children (cont'd)

Give us the strength to be poor with the poor, to be hap-py though our self-ish hearts cry out for more. When

Words: Sandy Boyce Music: Kathy Pike
Copyright © 1990 Sandy Boyce and Kathy Pike. Used by permission.

God is so good

17

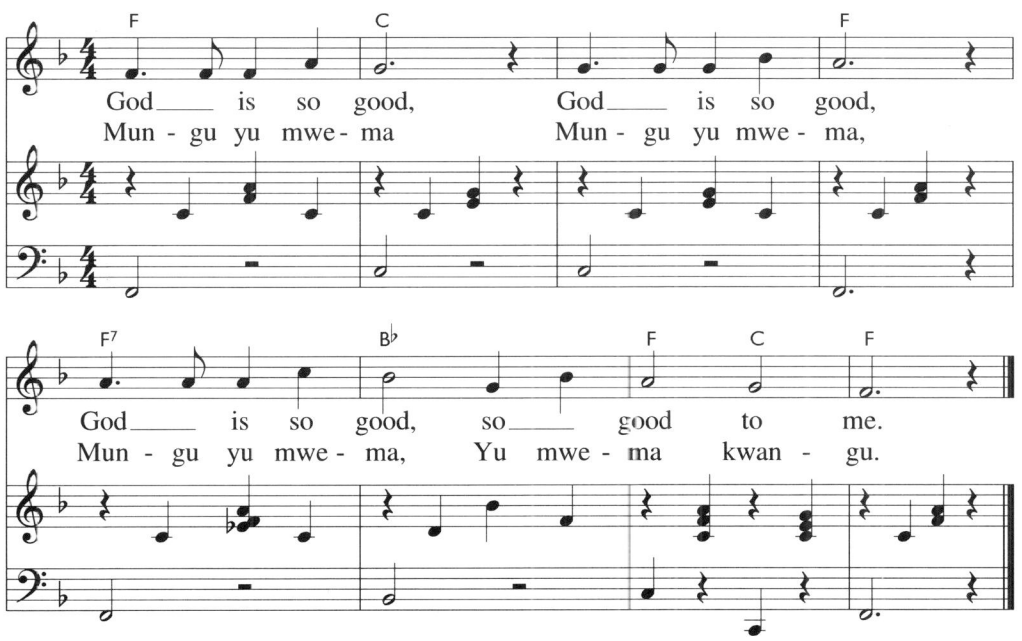

God is so good, God is so good,
Mun-gu yu mwe-ma, Mun-gu yu mwe-ma,
God is so good, so good to me.
Mun-gu yu mwe-ma, Yu mwe-ma kwan-gu.

Traditional, Swahili

This song can be very effective as a centering song after a particularly active time. Sing it several times and allow the children to experience God's goodness as they sing it. Make sure that the children know and understand the original Swahili words.

Rainbow Songbook

18 Growing in God's way

This is an excellent intergenerational song. It emphasizes the growth everyone, young and old, must go through.

1. "My, how you've grown," the woman said As she smiled and patted the top of my head, But I'm growing in ways that she didn't see, God's love is growing deep down inside me,
2. Fam-'ly and friends can sure make you mad, Loving is hard even for mom and dad, So we come together to learn and to pray, Helping each other to grow in God's way, And we're grow-
3. Water and sun help our gardens to grow, Also our work with the rake and the hoe, God is the gard'ner that cares for each one, Wat'ring and waiting for new growth to come,
4. We all make mistakes and then start anew, There's always much more to learn and to do, So that God's great Shalom will come shining through, Remember God's counting on me and on you,

Rainbow Songbook

Growing in God's way (cont'd)

ing, grow - ing, grow - ing ev - 'ry day. Yes, we're grow - ing, grow - ing, grow - ing in __ God's way.

Words: Jim Strathdee and Marilyn Perry
Music: Jim Strathdee
Copyright © 1989 Desert Flower Music. Used by permission.

Rainbow Songbook

19 Hands left and right

Hands left and right (cont'd)

Hands left and right (cont'd)

Words and music: Linnea Good.
Copyright © 1988 Borealis Music. Used by permission.

Halle, halle, hallelujah

Use this song as a chorus, repeating it a number of times. Add new percussion instruments each time you sing the verse. Varying the tempo will give this song a wider range of usefulness.

Traditional

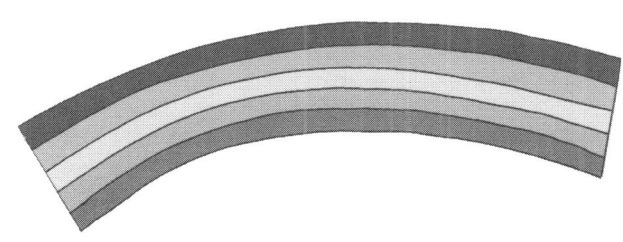

Rainbow Songbook

21 I am sent by God

Rainbow Songbook

I am sent by God (cont'd)

Words: trad. Cuban, English tr. Donald Schmidt
Music: trad. Cuban, arr. Alan Whitmore
English tr. and arr. copyright © Wood Lake Books.

22   I will sing, I will sing

A zipper song. The chorus may be sung after each verse or as a concluding verse at the end. Make up your own verses or use some of the following:

We will laugh...with God's joy in our hearts...

We will hope...for God's peace on the earth...

We will tell...good news about God's love...

We will dance...with joy and liberty...

Words: Max Dyer
Music: Betty Pulkingham and Max Dyer
Copyright © 1974 Celebration, (Administered by The Copyright Co., Nashville, TN).
All rights reserved. International copyright secured. Used by permission.

Jesus came a child like me

23

Words: Walter Farquharson
Music: Richard D. Hall
Words copyright © 1987 Walter Farquharson. Music copyright © 1988 Richard D. Hall.
Used by permission.

Rainbow Songbook

24 Jesus came bringing us

Add new verses as you wish.

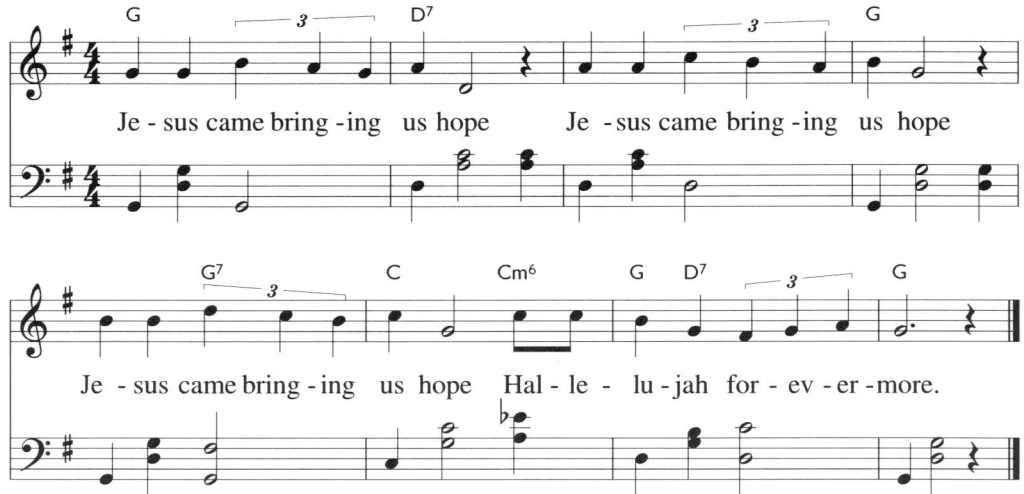

2. Jesus came showing God's peace...
3. Jesus came bringing us joy...
4. Jesus came showing God's love...
5. Jesus came showing justice...

Traditional Cameroon folk song

Rainbow Songbook

Jesus loves the little children/Dancing rainbows

Choose a color. Make colored streamers to match. During the verses of "Jesus Loves.." dance and wave the colored streams to make a "dancing rainbow." In the rest of the song, stand and sit as directed in the words.

Words and music: traditional and Lesley J. Clare.
Rev. vs. 1 Lesley J. Clare, vs. 2 Lesley J. Clare.
Vs. 1 revised words and vs. 2 words copyright © 1990 Lesley J. Clare.
Music copyright © Lesley J. Clare. Used by permission.

Rainbow Songbook

26 — Jesus put this song into our hearts

A fifth verse can be added using "Halle, halle, halle, hallelujah." This allows everyone to dance, clap, and be involved without the necessity of reading words.

Je-sus put this song in-to our hearts, it's a song of joy no one can take a-way.
Je-sus taught us how to live in har-mo-ny, dif-ferent fa-ces, dif-ferent ra-ces, he made us one.
Je-sus taught us how to be a fa-mi-ly, lov-ing one a-no-ther with the love that he gives.
Je-sus turned our sor-row in-to danc-ing, changed our tears of sad-ness in-to ri-vers of joy.

Je-sus put this song in-to our
Je-sus taught us how to live in har-mo-
Je-sus taught us how to be a fa-mi-
Je-sus turned our sor-rows in-to a

Rainbow Songbook

hearts.
ny.
ly.
dance.

Words and music: Graham Kendrick
Copyright © 1986 Thankyou Music ((Administered by EMI Christian Music Publishing), ASCAP.
Used by permission.

Kind hands

Je-sus' hands were kind hands, do-ing good to all.
Take my hands, Lord Je-sus, let them work for you.

Heal-ing pain and sick-ness, bless-ing child-ren small.
Make them strong and gen-tle, kind in all I do.

Wash-ing tir-ed feet and sav-ing those who fall.
Let me watch you, Je-sus, till I'm gen-tle too.

Je-sus' hands were kind hands, do-ing good to all.
Till my hands are kind hands, quick to work for you.

Old French melody
Words: Margaret Cropper
Copyright © Estate of Margaret Cropper. Used by permission.

28 Let's talk

A zipper song. Create your own verses.

Additional verses: Let's talk about what Jesus has taught...
Let's talk about the good news we've heard...
Let's talk about how lives have been changed...
Let's talk about the wonders we've seen...
Let's go out to tell the good news...

Words and music: Donald Schmidt, arr. Michael Bloss
Copyright © 1997 Wood Lake Books.

Light one candle

29

Words and music: Natalie Sleeth
Copyright © 1976 Hinshaw Music, Inc.
Used by permission.

Love the Lord your God

Words and music: Jim & Jean Strathdee
Copyright © 1991 Desert Flower Music. Used by permission.

 Love
 God
 with

 heart
 soul
 mind

 all that you are

Rainbow Songbook

31 Living in the light

Living in the light (cont'd)

it hurts our eyes to see the glow.
a star is there to light our way.
He showed us things we had-n't seen.
and let us rise to see the dawn.

Some-times a word of hope re-minds us of our
It tells a sto-ry of Je-sus who came
Now we, like Je-sus, can help cre-a-tion
We trust that God is here a - spar-kle and a-

fears, our mem-or-ies and tears.
near to say: "God's light will ev-er stay."
shine, and this will be a sign:
blaze, warm-ing all our days.

Words and music: Linnea Good
Copyright © 1992 Borealis Music. Used by permission.

32
Light up the candle/Blow out the candle

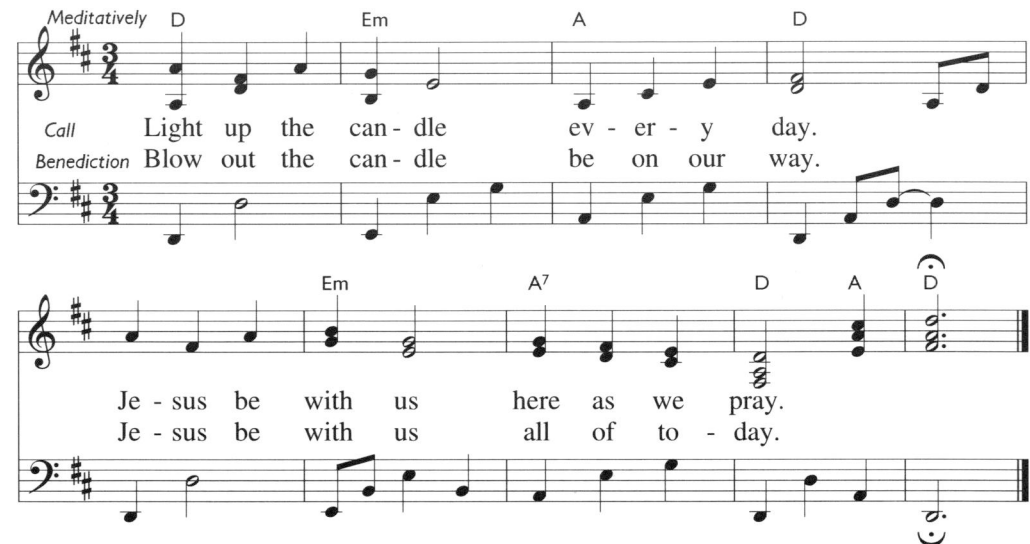

Call Light up the candle ev-er-y day.
Benediction Blow out the candle be on our way.
Je-sus be with us here as we pray.
Je-sus be with us all of to-day.

Words and music: David and Danielle Mills
Copyright © 1992 Danielle and David Mills. Used by permission.

33
Love, love, love your God

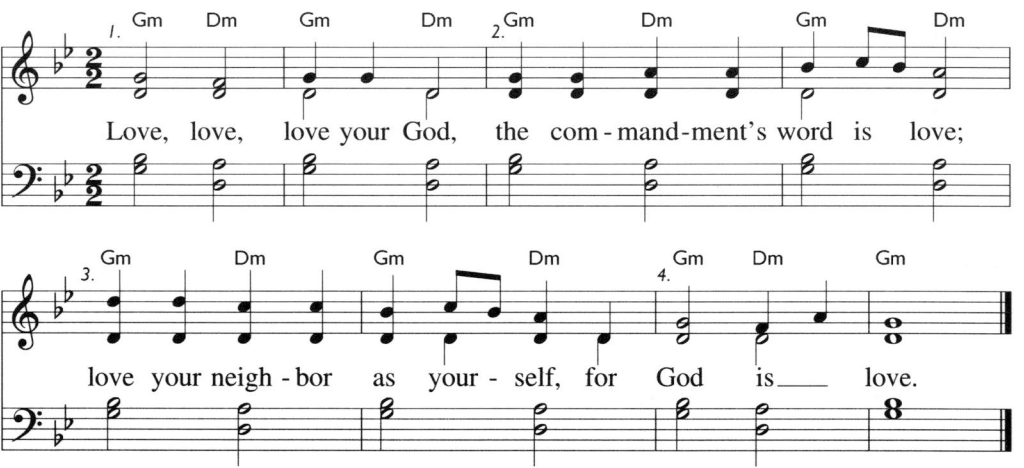

Love, love, love your God, the com-mand-ment's word is love;
love your neigh-bor as your-self, for God is love.

Traditional

Rainbow Songbook

Love, love, love! That's what 34

Love, love, love!
Peace, peace, peace!
Joy, joy, joy! That's what it's all a-bout! 'Cause God loves us, we
Me, me, me!
You, you, you!

love each oth-er, moth-er, fa-ther, sis-ter, broth-er

Ev-'ry-bod-y sing and shout 'cause that's what it's all a-

bout!
It's a-bout love, love, love! It's a-bout love, love, love!
It's a-bout peace, peace, peace! It's a-bout peace, peace, peace!
It's a-bout joy, joy, joy! It's a-bout joy, joy, joy!
It's a-bout me, me, me! It's a-bout me, me, me!
It's a-bout you, you, you! It's a-bout you! you! you!

Words and music: Lois & Herbert Brokering
Copyright © 1970 Augsburg Publishing House. Reprinted by permission of Augsburg Fortress.

Rainbow Songbook

35 Magic penny

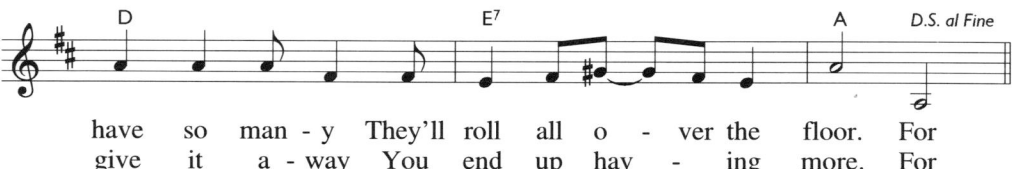

Chorus: Love is some-thing if you give it a-way, Give it a-way, give it a-way. Love is some-thing if you give it a-way, You end up hav-ing more. It's just like a mag-ic pen-ny

So let's go dancing 'til the break of day
Hold on tight and you won't have a-ny. Lend it, spend it and you'll
If there's a pi-per we can pay For love is some-thing if you
have so man-y They'll roll all o-ver the floor. For
give it a-way You end up hav-ing more. For

Words and music: Malvina Reynolds
Copyright © 1955, 1959 Universal-Northern Music Company.
Copyright renewed. Rights administered by Universal-MCA Music Publishing, a division of Universal Studios, Inc.
All rights reserved. Used by permission of Warner Bros. Publications U.S. Inc.

Love

Give it away ...
Lend it

Give it away ...
Spend it

More

Hold it tight

Many

Roll all over the floor

Rainbow Songbook

May the hope of God

36

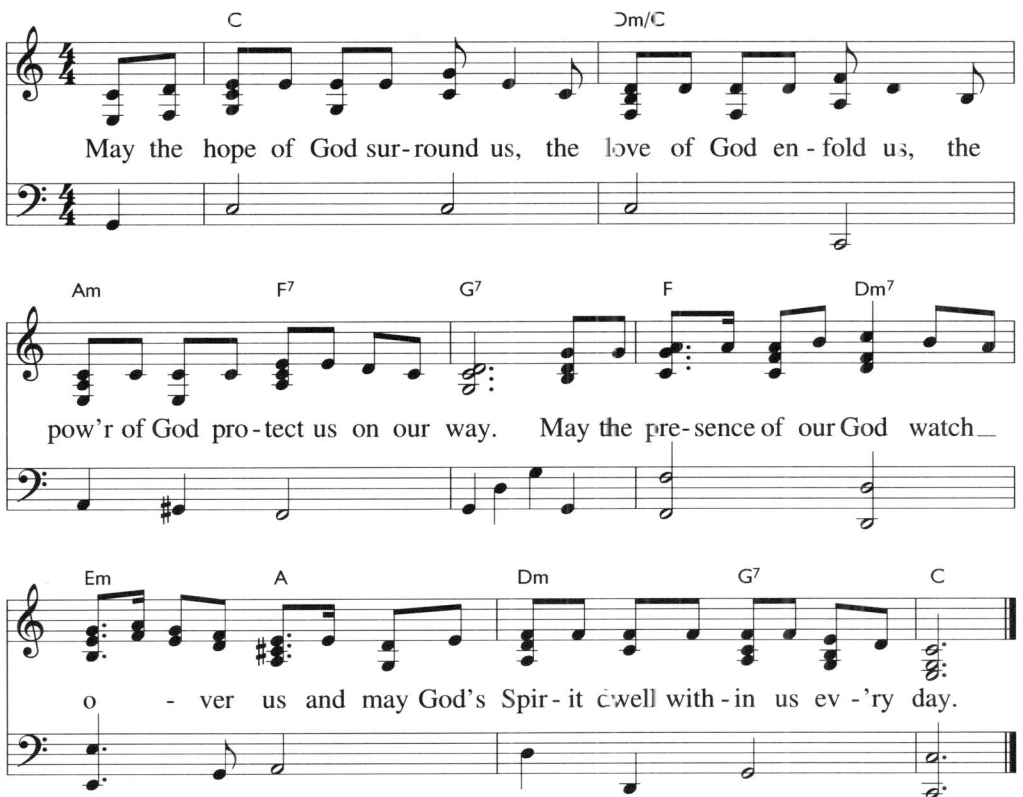

Words: The Whole People of God
Music: Donald Schmidt
Arr. Michael Bloss
Copyright © 1997 Wood Lake Books.

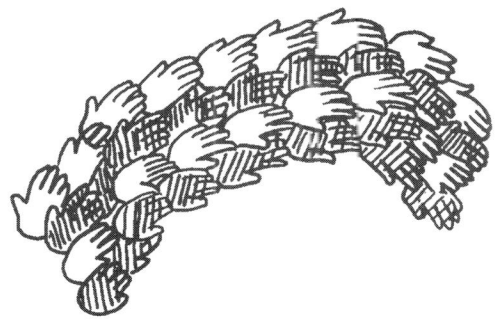

Rainbow Songbook

37 Come into God's presence

Sing this as a unison song or as a round.

Come in-to God's pres-ence sing-ing, "Al-le-lu-ia, al-le-lu-ia, al-le-lu-ia."

Additional verses: Come into God's presence singing: Joy to the world.
Songs that will heal.
Hope for the earth.
Love is the way.
Glory to God.

Traditional

38 My promise

Af-ter dark and stor-my weath-er To No-ah and his fa-mi-ly and to ev-'ry liv-ing crea-ture God makes a cov-e-nant and says My pro-mise is for love My pro-mise is for-

Now when A-bra-ham and Sar-ah packed up all of their be-long-ings for a brand new way of liv-ing it was be-cause they heard God's call My pro-mise is for love My pro-mise is for-

Mo-ses led the He-brew peo-ple out of slav-'ry in-to free-dom they need-ed rules to help them live in peace So Mo-ses told them what God said My pro-mise is for love My pro-mise is for-

In the days of man-y pro-phets Peo-ple turned their backs on God's way Used their lips for faith but not their hands Till Je-re-mi-ah heard God say My pro-mise is for love My pro-mise is for-

My promise (cont'd)

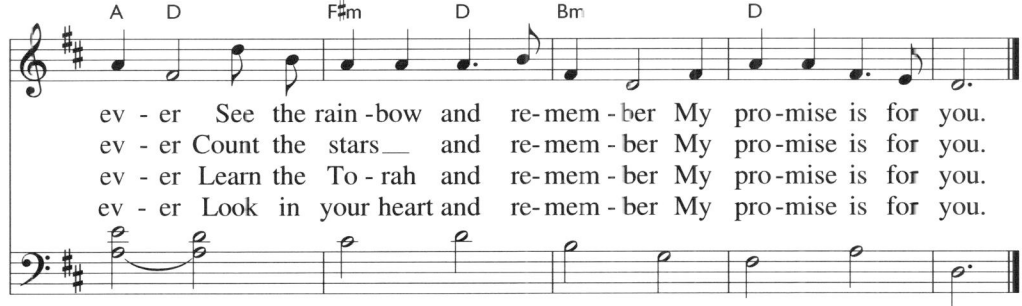

ev - er See the rain-bow and re-mem-ber My pro-mise is for you.
ev - er Count the stars__ and re-mem-ber My pro-mise is for you.
ev - er Learn the To - rah and re-mem-ber My pro-mise is for you.
ev - er Look in your heart and re-mem-ber My pro-mise is for you.

Peter, Mary and the others
Heard that Jesus soon would leave them
They were confused and frightened people
So Jesus gently said to them
My promise is for love
My promise is forever
Eat the bread and remember
My promise is for you.

Dear God, may the words on my lips
and the thoughts that are in my heart
and the actions of my hands and feet
be a pleasing gift to you
My promise is for love
My promise is forever
Look at me God and remember
My promise is for you.

Words and music: Lesley J. Clare
Copyright © 1995 Lesley J. Clare. Used by permission.

Opening song/Closing song

39

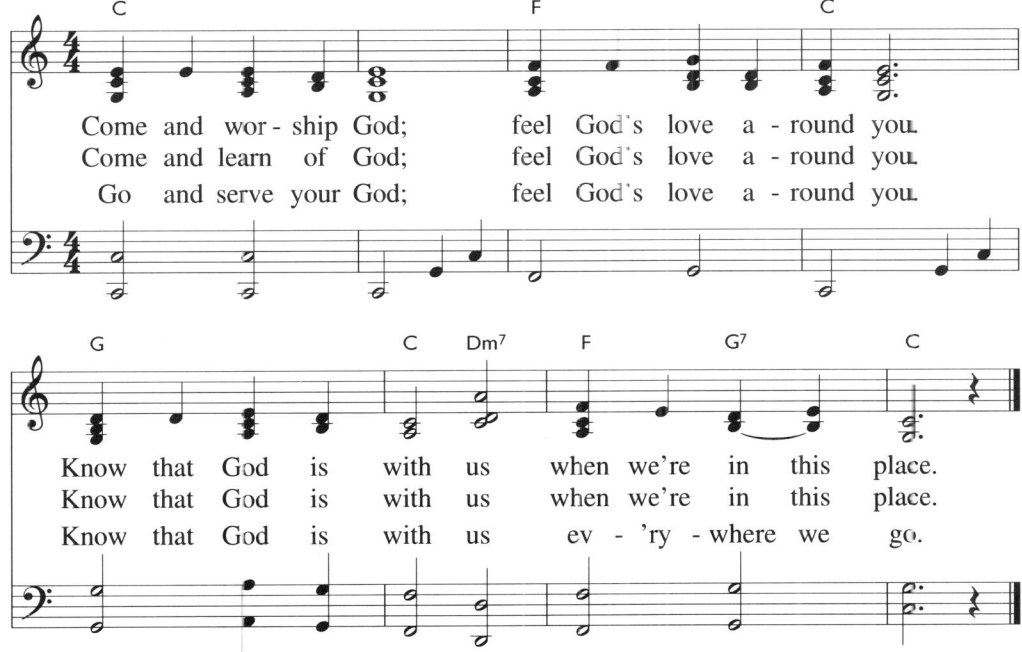

Come and wor-ship God; feel God's love a-round you.
Come and learn of God; feel God's love a-round you.
Go and serve your God; feel God's love a-round you.

Know that God is with us when we're in this place.
Know that God is with us when we're in this place.
Know that God is with us ev-'ry-where we go.

Words and music: Donald Schmidt, arr. Micahel Bloss
Words and music copyright © 1995 Donald Schmidt.
Arr. Copyright © 1998 Wood Lake Books.

Rainbow Songbook

40 — My peace

This is a zipper song. To create additional verses please replace "peace" with "joy" and "love".

My ___ peace I ___ give un-to you;
It's a peace that the world can-not give.
It's a peace that the world can-not un-der-stand; peace to know, peace to live, My ___ peace I give un-to you.

Words and music: Keith Routledge
Copyright © 1975 Sovereign Music UK. Used by permission.

One more step

One more step a-long the world I go. One more step a-long the world I go. From the old things to the new Keep me tra-vel-ing a-long with You.

Round the cor-ner of the world I turn. More and more a-bout the world I learn. All the new things that I see You'll be look-ing at a-long with me.

As I tra-vel through the bad and good. Keep me tra-vel-ing the way I should. Where I see no way to go You'll be tell-ing me the way, I know. And it's from the old I tra-vel to the new. Keep me tra-vel-ing a-long with You.

Give me cour-age when the world is rough. Keep me lov-ing though the world is tough. Leap and sing in all I do. Keep me tra-vel-ing a-long with You.

You are old-er than the world can be. You are young-er than the life in me. Ev-er old and ev-er new. Keep me tra-vel-ing a-long with You.

Words and music: Sydney Carter
Copyright © 1971, 1974 Stainer & Bell Ltd.
Admin. in N.A. by Hope Publishing Co., Carol Stream, IL 60188. All rights reserved.
Used by permission of Hope Publishing Co. and Stainer and Bell Ltd., London, England.

42 Oh, what a wonderful gift

The use of drums will greatly enhance the presentation of this song.

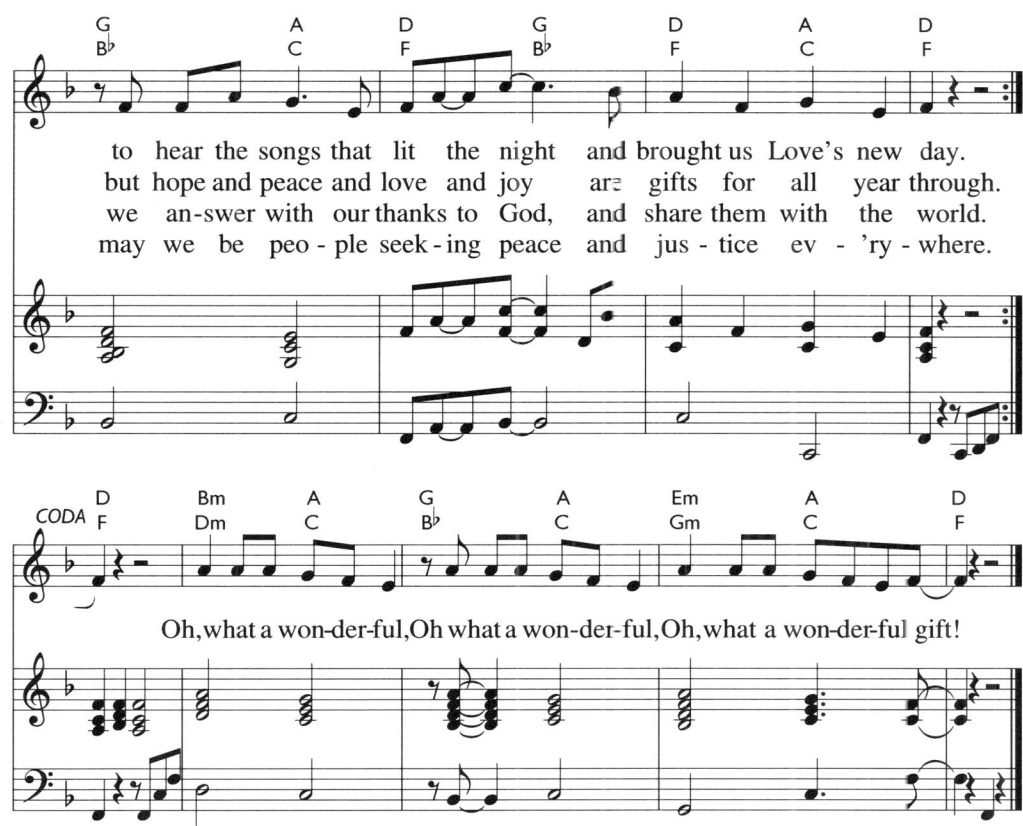

Words and music: Linnea Good
Copyright © 1992 Borealis Music. Used by permission.

43 Part of the family

Rainbow Songbook

Part of the family (cont'd)

4. We can be noisy or quiet as mice
   Our tempers flare up or we're colder than ice
   Sometimes we're grumpy when we want to be nice
   But we are part of the family.
   We try to be loving but often we find
   We're rude when we're saying just what's on our mind.
   God teach us a way that's both honest and kind
   For we are a part of your family.

Words and music: Jim Manley
Copyright © 1984 James K. Manley. Used by permission.

44 Make a joyful noise

Make a joyful noise (cont'd)

Psalm 100
Words and music: Linnea Good
Copyright © 1992 Borealis Music. Used by permission.

45 Rejoice in the Lord always

This song can be sung in unison or as a round.

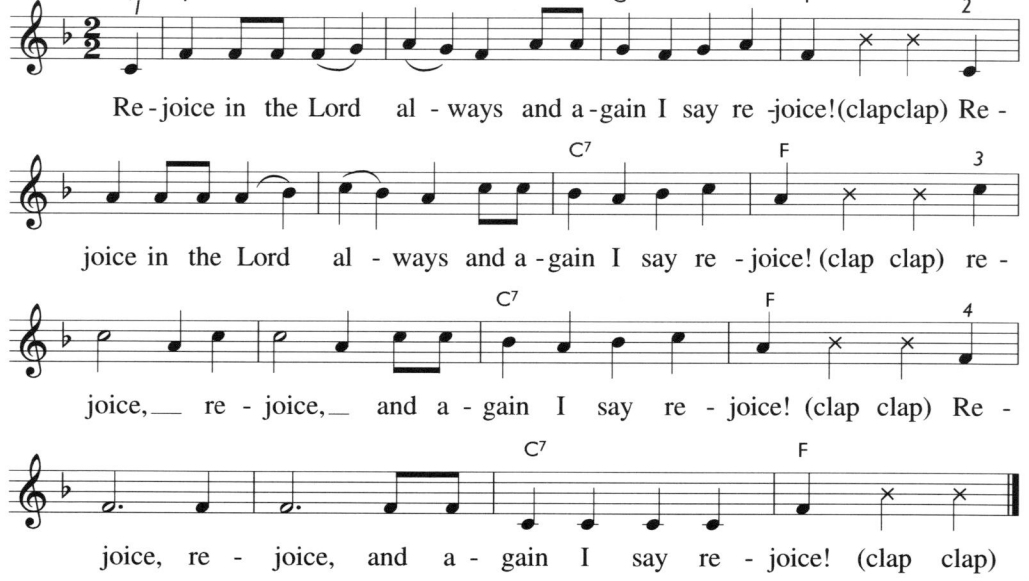

Traditional

46 Shalom

This song can be sung in unison or as a round. The round may be in three different ways, using 1, 2, 3, 4; a, b, c, d; or A, B.

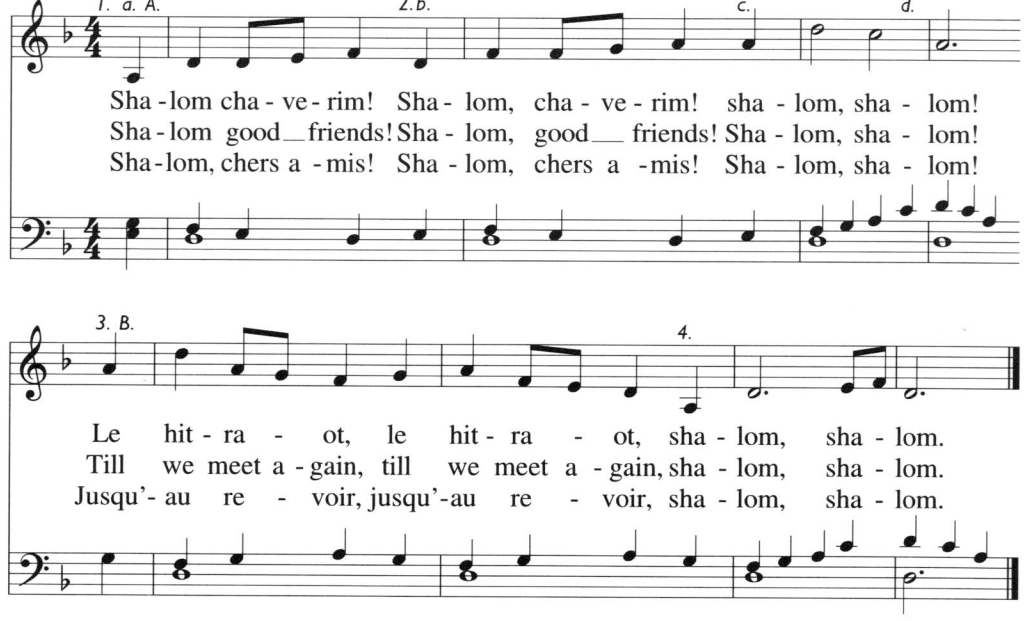

Israeli round

Sing alleluia

47

Peo - ple, all, come sing and shout; God is in us dwell - ing.
Ev - ery one a child of God, sis - ter or a broth - er.
For the gifts that we re - ceive, come with thank - ful giv - ing.

Spread the joy - ful news a - bout; sing with voic - es swell - ing.
All who know the love of God, share with one an - oth - er.
Let the pro - mise we be - lieve light the life we're liv - ing.

Refrain
Sing al - le - lu - ia, sing al - le - lu - ia;
raise your voic - es, shout with joy; sing praise to God, the Sav - ior.

Words and music: Sue Ellen Page, rev. words: Eric Johnson, rev. music: Sue Ellen Page
Copyright © 1968 and 1986 Choristers Guild.
Used by permission.

Rainbow Songbook

48 Simple gifts

Traditional Shaker hymn, 1848

The Shakers, a group that formed from the Quakers, was a Christian group that got their name from the way they moved when they danced. Their faith and joy was expressed by their dancing which sometimes resembled Native dances. The Shakers' commitment to a simple life is reflected in their hymn "Simple Gifts." Although there were 4000 Shakers in 1845, by the beginning of the 1900s they had begun to disappear as a religious group. This group, remembered for their beautiful furniture and for their dancing, is found now in only two communities in Maine and New Hampshire.

ACTIONS

(With hands joined, make a circle.)

'Tis the gift to be simple
(Circle left with bodies turned left. On "simple" bend right leg.)

'Tis the gift to be free
(Circle right with bodies turned right. On "free" bend left leg.)

'Tis the gift that comes 'round where we ought to be.
(Repeat above actions.)

And when we find ourselves in the place just right
(Facing center with hands joined and slowly raising arms, walk into the center.)

It will be in the valley of love and delight.
(Walk back to circle, still holding hands and slowly lowering arms.)

When true simplicity is gained
(Clap hands on each beat, begin clapping at your lower right side, continue up and around above your head and finish at your left side.)

To bow and to bend, we will not be ashamed.
(Bend at the waist facing the center of the circle with arms outstretched, palms down, then stand up, arms outstretched.)

To turn and to turn will be our delight
'Til by turning, turning, we come 'round right.
(Move feet and body in 1/4 turns, clapping low and then high at each turn. The fourth 1/4 turn should return you to your original position.)

Rainbow Songbook

49 Ten commandments

Get smaller children to hold up fingers or numbered cards as the commandments are being sung.

Moses climbed the mountain high,
God spoke to Moses from the cloud of smoke.
Lightning flashed and the mountain shook and thundered when God spoke.
Ten commandments God did give, to you and me to

Number one says WORSHIP GOD
Number two says MAKE NO OTHER GODS.
Number three, RESPECT GOD'S NAME, DON'T USE IT CARELESSLY.
Number four says TAKE ONE DAY TO REST, AND HONOR

Number five saye LOVE YOUR MOM AND DAD
Number six says DON'T KILL ANYONE.
Seven says BE FAITHFUL TO EACH OTHER WHEN YOU'RE A PARTNER FOR LIFE.
Number eight says DO NOT STEAL, Nine says DON'T TELL

Rainbow Songbook

Ten commandments (cont'd)

help us live that we may learn to
ALL GOD MADE, so ev'-ry week we
LIES A-BOUT EACH OTH-ER, Num-ber ten says

love our God, and live to-geth-er in peace.
work and play and wor-ship on the Sab-bath day.
DO NOT WANT TO TAKE WHAT BE-LONGS TO AN-OTH-ER.

Chorus

Ten com-mand-ments God did give, to you and me to help us live, that

we may learn to love our God, and live to-geth-er in peace.

Words and music: Jean and Jim Strathdee
Copyright © 1991 Desert Flower Music. Used by permission.

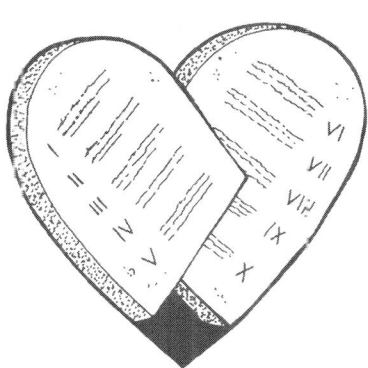

Rainbow Songbook

50

Thank God

A good zipper song. Add verses by substituting the words Serve God, Praise God, Love God, etc. Create your own verses.

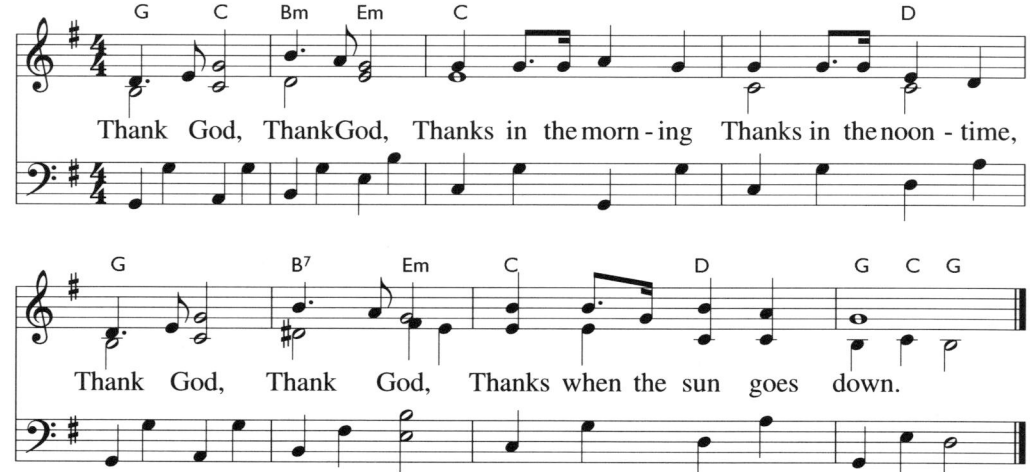

Traditional

51

The spirit in me

Sing through a number of times, increasing the volume and amount of accompaniment with each repetition.

Words and music: Jim Strathdee
Copyright © 1972 Desert Flower Music. Used by permission.

The whole world   52

The whole world is in God's hands, the whole world in lov-ing
Birds and bees are in God's hands,___ birds and bees in lov-ing
You and me, we're in God's hands,___ you and me, in lov-ing

hands, the whole world is in God's hands, the world is in God's hands.
hands,___ birds and bees are in God's hands, the world is in God's hands.
hands,___ you and me we're in God's hands, the world is in God's hands.

This is a good zipper song. Have the singers mime the things mentioned in each verse.

Add your own verses. Some suggestions:

Flowers and trees...
Elephants and fleas...
The little baby is...
Mommies and Daddies...
Grandma and Grandpa...
Monsters and mice...
(Name) and (Name)...

Words: traditional, rev. Lesley J. Clare
Music: traditional
Rev. words copyright © Lesley J. Clare. Used by permission.

Rainbow Songbook

53 The people of God

The peo-ple of God in the de-sert long wan-dered,
sus-tained by a pre-sence that bec-koned them on-ward.
They bore just their hope and the dust of the high-way.

The peo-ple of God some-times turned back in an-ger.
The high cost of lov-ing they could not sus-tain.
The peo-ple of God through their tears asked for par-don
Raised their heads, squared their shoul-ders and set off a-gain.

The peo-ple of God on their jour-ney knew hun-ger.
You fed them with man-na sent down from a-bove.
The peo-ple of God with thanks-giv-ing and won-der,
Were cared for and nour-ished by your in-fin-ite love.

The peo-ple of God with a long way to go,
Caught a glimpse of the coun-try God had planned for their home.
The peo-ple of God raised their voic-es in sing-ing
The sound of their prais-es set the de-sert to ring-ing.

Rainbow Songbook

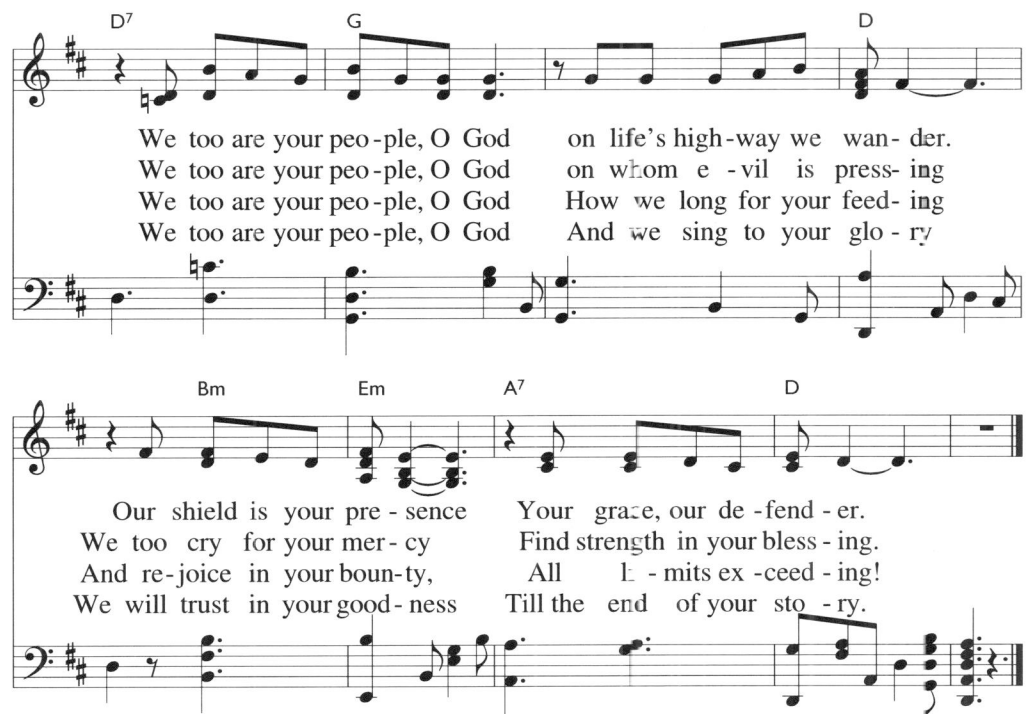

Words and music: trad. Brazilian
Eng. trans: Judith A. Fetter
English translation copyright © 1994 Judith A. Fetter. Used by permission.

54   The whole people of God

Come in-to our church and see who is there, The chil-dren are danc-ing there's a song in the air. Grand-ma is sit-ting in her fa-vor-ite chair and it's high time to wor-ship our God. For all of God's chil-dren we o-pen the door, The young and the old and the rich and the poor, We all come to-geth-er our lives to re-

We o-pen the Book our sto-ries to tell Of Mar-y and Jo-seph, we know them so well, From Ad-vent to Pen-te-cost weav-ing their spell, What a fine way to learn of our God. We know that God's pres-ence is with us to-day Help-ing and guid-ing our work and our play. Love and for-give-ness will show us the

Sun-day school's done, the church serv-ice ends, It's time to go home to our fam-'ly and friends, And share with each oth-er the love God in-tends, It's a great day for serv-ing our God. We love God's cre-a-tion each flow-er and tree, Mend bro-ken hearts, help the cap-tives go free, We grow towards the full-ness of all we can

Rainbow Songbook

The whole people of God (cont'd)

Words and music: Jim Strathdee
Copyright © 1989 Desert Flower Music. Used by permission.

55 This is my commandment

Words and music: traditional, arr. Jim Strathdee
Copyright © 1994 Jim Strathdee. Used by permission.

Walk in the Light

56

1. & 4. Walk in the Light. Loved in God's sight. Thru the long night, Walk, walk in the Light. (4) Walk in the Light.
2. Come take my hand, Heal this scarred land, To-geth-er we'll stand, Come, come take my hand.
3. We're not a-lone, left on our own, loved as God's own. We're, we're not a-lone.

Words and music: Jim Strathdee
Copyright © 1994 Desert Flower Music. Used by permission.

Rainbow Songbook

57 Turning of the world

Turning of the world (cont'd)

Words and music: Ruth Pelham
Copyright © 1982 Ruth Pelham ASCAP. Used by permission.

58 Walk with me

Words and music: John S. Rice
Copyright © 1994 Estate of John S. Rice. Used by permission.

We are the church

59

I am the church! You are the church! We are the church together!
All who follow Jesus, All around the world! Yes, we're the church together!

The church is not a building, The church is not a steeple, The church is not a resting place, The church is a people!
We're many kinds of people With many kinds of faces, All colors and all ages, too From all times and places.
And when the people gather, There's singing and there's praying, There's laughing and there's crying sometimes, All of it saying:
I count if I am ninety, Or nine or just a baby; There's one thing I am sure about And I don't mean maybe:

Words and music: Richard Avery & Donald Marsh
Copyright © 1972 by Hope Publishing Company, Carol Stream, IL 60188. All rights reserved. Used by permission.
Artwork copyright © Wood Lake Books.

I am

church

you are

Jesus

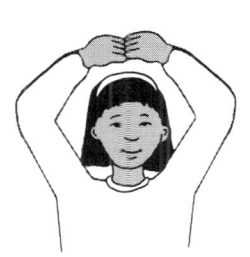
all around the world

we are the church together

Rainbow Songbook

60 Who is a disciple?

Who is a disciple? Look and you will see. Those who follow Jesus learning what to be. Mary Magdalene was one she walked close by our Lord. And was the first to find him ris'n, on that Easter morn.

Who is a disciple? Look and you will see. Four strong men out fishing the Sea of Galilee. Peter, Andrew, James and John left their nets behind And followed Jesus just to know God's love for humankind. Jesus, Jesus

Who is a disciple? Look and you will see. A woman with a jar of oil anointing lovingly. With tender tears she bathed his feet, gave love complete and bold. And Jesus said, "For evermore, your story will be told."

Who is a disciple? Look and you will see. People all around us they look like you and me. When we learn to love and share, care for everyone, We become disciples too and Jesus' work is done.

teach me how to be a disciple of your love for all the world to see.

Words and music: Jean Strathdee
Copyright © 1990 Desert Flower Music. Used by permission.

Three psalm settings   61

Ps. 85:10
Words and music: Donald Schmidt
Copyright © 1997 Wood Lake Books.

Ps. 145:2
Words and music: Donald Schmidt
Copyright © 1997 Wood Lake Books.

Ps. 126:3
Words and music: Donald Schmidt
Copyright © 1997 Wood Lake Books.

Rainbow Songbook

62 What does the Lord require?

This song can be sung two ways. The first, and possibly most effective way, is to teach each musical line to one group of people. Begin with the third part (men), and add the second (alto) and first (soprano) on successive repetitions. Once all the parts are together, sing it a number of times. The song may also be sung in its entirety as a round.

Soprano: To seek justice, and love kindness, and walk humbly with your God. God.

Alto: Justice, kindness, walk humbly with your God. God.

Men: What does the Lord require of you? What does the Lord require of you? you?

Words: Micah 6:8 Music: Jim Strathdee
Copyright © 1986 Desert Flower Music. Used by permission.

You gotta love

63

Words: Donald Schmidt
Music: traditional, arr. Michael Bloss
Words copyright © 1995 Donald Schmidt.
Arr. copyright © 1998 Wood Lake Books.

Rainbow Songbook

Index of Topics & Categories

Action Song
  Clap Your Hands 3
  Come Lord Jesus 4
  God Is Here 13
  Love the Lord Your God 30
  Magic Penny 35
  We Are the Church 59

Baptism
  God Is Here 13
  Part of the Family 43

Benediction/Sending Forth
  Blow Out the Candle 32
  Closing Song 39
  Go Now in Peace 14
  I Am Sent by God 21
  Leaving Song 2
  May the Hope 36
  My Peace 40
  Shalom 46
  The Whole People of God 54
  Walk in the Light 56
  Walk with Me 58

Bible Story
  My Promise 38

Call to Prayer
  Come, Lord Jesus 4

Call to Worship/Gathering
  Arriving Song 1
  Come into God's Presence 37
  Come, Lord Jesus 4
  Dance with the Spirit 6
  Draw the Circle Wide 5
  Everything We Need 9
  Give Glory to God 11
  God Is Here 13
  Light Up the Candle 32
  Love, Love, Love! That's What 34
  Make a Joyful Noise 44
  Opening Song 39

  Part of the Family 43
  Shalom 46
  The Spirit in Me 51
  The Whole People of God 54
  We Are the Church 59

Church Season

ADVENT
  Come, Lord Jesus 4
  Get Ready 10
  Jesus Came Bringing Us 24
  Light One Candle 29
  Oh, What a Wonderful Gift 42

CHRISTMAS
  Jesus Came Bringing Us 24
  Oh What a Wonderful Gift 42

EPIPHANY
  God Is Like... 15
  Living in the Light 31
  Oh, What a Wonderful Gift 42

LENT
  God Sees the Children 16
  My Peace 40
  My Promise 38

EASTER
  Come into God's Presence 37
  Every Morning Is Easter Morning 7
  Halle, Halle, Hallelujah 20
  Jesus Put This Song into Our Hearts 26
  Sing Alleluia 47

PENTECOST
  Dance with the Spirit 6
  Magic Penny 35
  My Peace 40
  The Spirit in Me 51

REIGN OF CHRIST
  My Peace 40

Communion/Holy Eucharist
  Draw the Circle Wide 5
  God Is Like... 15
  My Peace 40
  My Promise 38
  Part of the Family 43

Creation
  Draw the Circle Wide 5
  Everything We Need 9
  Glory to God 12
  The Whole World 52

Discipleship
  Jesus Came a Child Like Me 23

Faith
  God Is So Good 17
  Growing in God's Way 18
  Jesus Put This Song into Our Hearts 26

Family
  God Is Like... 15
  Growing in God's Way 18
  Love, Love, Love! That's What 34

God's Nature
  God Is Here 13
  God Is Like... 15
  God Is So Good 17
  God Sees the Children 16
  Love, Love, Love Your God 33
  One More Step 41

Grace
  From You I Receive 8
  God Is Here 13
  This Is My Commandment 55

Jesus
  Jesus Came a Child Like Me 23
  Jesus Came Bringing Us 24
  Jesus Loves the Little Children/
      Dancing Rainbows 25
  Kind Hands 27
  Let's Talk 28
  Living in the Light 31
  My Peace 40

Journey
  Growing in God's Way 18
  May the Hope 36
  One More Step 41
  Simple Gifts 48
  The People of God 53
  Walk in the Light 56
  Walk with Me 58

Peace/Justice
  Dance with the Spirit 6
  Draw the Circle Wide 5
  Give Glory to God 11
  God Sees the Children 16
  Hands Left and Right 19
  I Am Sent by God 21
  Love the Lord Your God 30
  Magic Penny 35
  My Promise 38
  Oh, What a Wonderful Gift 42
  Shalom 46
  Three Psalm Settings 61
  Turning of the World 57
  Walk in the Light 56
  Walk with Me 58
  What Does the Lord Require? 62

Praise
  Clap Your Hands 3
  Come into God's Presence 37
  Every Morning Is Easter Morning 7
  Everything We Need 9
  Give Glory to God 11
  Glory to God 12
  God Is So Good 17
  Halle, Halle, Hallelujah 20
  I Will Sing, I Will Sing 22
  Jesus Put This Song into Our Hearts 26
  Magic Penny 35
  Make a Joyful Noise 44
  Rejoice in the Lord Always 45
  Sing Alleluia 47
  Thank God 50
  The Whole World 52
  Three Psalm Settings 61

Prayer Response
- Give Glory to God **11**
- God Is So Good **17**
- Halle, Halle, Hallelujah **20**
- May the Hope **36**
- This Is My Commandment **55**
- What Does the Lord Require? **62**
- You Gotta Love **63**

Scriptural Reference
- Gn 9:1–17, My Promise **38**
- Gn 12:1–3, My Promise **38**
- Ex 20:1–17, My Promise **38**
  - Ten Commandments **49**
- Deut 5:1–21, My Promise **38**
  - Ten Commandments **49**
- Deut 6:5, Love the Lord Your God **30**
  - You Gotta Love **63**
- Ps 85, Three Psalm Settings **61**
- Ps 100, Make a Joyful Noise **44**
- Ps 126, Three Psalm Settings **61**
- Ps 145, Three Psalm Settings **61**
- Ps 150, Clap Your Hands **3**
- Is 60:1, Oh, What a Wonderful Gift **42**
- Jer 1:4–10, My Promise **38**
- Mic 6:8, Ten Commandments **49**
  - What Does the Lord Require? **62**
- Mt 3:1–12, Get Ready **10**
- Mt 4:18–22, Who Is a Disciple? **60**
- Mt 22:37, Love the Lord Your God **30**
- Mt 22:37–39, You Gotta Love **63**
- Mt 26:6–13, Who Is a Disciple? **60**
- Mt 26:26–30, My Promise **38**
- Mk 1:1–8, Get Ready **10**
- Mk 1:16–20, Who Is a Disciple? **60**
- Mk 12:30, Love the Lord Your God **30**
- Mk 12:30–31, You Gotta Love **63**
- Mk 14:3–9, Who Is a Disciple? **60**
- Mk 14:22–26, My Promise **38**
- Lk 1:26–38, Get Ready **10**
- Lk 3:1–17, Get Ready **10**
- Lk 5:1–11, Who Is a Disciple? **60**
- Lk 10:27, Love the Lord Your God **30**
  - You Gotta Love **63**
- Lk 15:11–32, God Is Like… **15**
- Lk 22:14–23, My Promise **38**
- Jn 1:19–28, Get Ready **10**
- Jn 13:34, This Is My Commandment **55**
- Jn 14:27, My Peace **40**
- Jn 16:22, Give Glory to God **11**
- Jn 20:11–18, Who Is a Disciple? **60**
- Phil 4:4–7, Rejoice in the Lord Always **45**

Service
- God Sees the Children **16**
- Hands Left and Right **19**
- Thank God **50**
- The Whole People of God **54**
- Turning of the World **57**
- What Does the Lord Require? **62**
- Who Is a Disciple? **60**

Thanksgiving
- Everything We Need **9**
- From You I Receive **8**
- God Is So Good **17**
- Magic Penny **35**
- Oh, What a Wonderful Gift **42**
- Sing Alleluia **47**
- Thank God **50**

Witness
- Dance with the Spirit **6**
- Give Glory to God **11**
- God Sees the Children **16**
- I Am Sent by God **21**
- I Will Sing, I Will Sing **22**
- Let's Talk **28**
- Living in the Light **31**
- Love, Love, Love Your God **33**
- Magic Penny **35**
- We Are the Church **59**
- Who Is a Disciple? **60**
- You Gotta Love **63**

Other music resources available from the publishers of the Rainbow Songbook

Please note: all prices listed are Canadian dollars.

Printed Music

SPIRIT ANEW
EDITED BY ALAN C. WHITMORE
More than 175 songs help you connect with worship in time-honored ways. Includes praise choruses, scripture songs, meditative songs, prayer responses, mantras, African-American songs, songs for Communion and more.
Music Leader Edition • $39.95 • 1-55145-343-6
Pew Edition • $12.95 • 1-55145-345-2

SONGS FOR A GOSPEL PEOPLE
This popular hymnbook reflects an ecumenical, worldwide heritage. Over 400,000 copies sold.
Paper, coil • $8.95 • 0-919599-44-3

SPIRIT OF SINGING
MARDI TINDAL & KATE MIDDLETON
A collection of songs from a variety of traditions – perfect for around the campfire, at home or with community.
Paper • $8.95 • 0-92932-85-3

ALL GOD'S CHILDREN SING
A broad selection of music for children and intergenerational singing.
Paper • $24.95 • 0-919599-97-4
Cassette set • $29.95 • License available

HYMNS WE LOVE TO SING – LARGE PRINT
EDITED BY ALAN C. WHITMORE
Old and new favorites in an easier-to-see format.
Words and Music Edition • $29.95 • 1-55145-152-2
Words-Only • $9.95 • 1-55145-151-4

Recorded Music

RAINBOW SING-ALONG
Music for young children. Complements *The Whole People of God* lectionary curriculum resource.
Two Cassette Set • $19.95 • 1-55145-185-9
Compact Disk • $19.95 • 1-55145-199-9

SING A SONG OF SEASONS
LESLEY J. CLARE
Share these songs with your children. Book is available.
Cassette • $12.99 • 1-55145-147-6

I'M GOD'S CHILD
LESLEY J. CLARE
Fun sing-along tape and booklet for children 2 to 8 years old.
Cassette & Book • $19.95 • 0-929032-26-8

A large selection of recorded music from the Strathdees, Manley, and many others is available. Please contact Wood Lake Books for a complete list of titles.

Copyright Cleared Music for Churches & Congregations

Enrich your liturgy with copyright-cleared music for churches. The *LicenSing* program offers access to over 100,000 songs and hymns to churches for use in worship, church activities and community gatherings. For a low annual fee and a little simple record keeping, *LicenSing* clears the way for you to use a wealth of old favorites, contemporary hymns and an ever-expanding collection of new music.

There are many options available within the *LicenSing Music Program*, including special licenses for small congregations, camps, presbyteries and dioceses.

Please call toll-free for more information: In Canada – Wood Lake Books Inc. **1.800.663.2775**
In the USA - Logos Productions **1.800.328.0200** • In Australia – MediaCom Associates **1.800.811.311**
In New Zealand – MediaCom Associates **0800.833.477**
or write to: Wood Lake Books Inc., 9025 Jim Bailey Rd, Kelowna, BC Canada V4V 1R2